Food or Famine
Christopher Gibb
363.8

FOOD OR FAMINE?

Christopher Gibb

Rourke Enterprises, Inc.
Vero Beach, FL, 32964

World Issues

Food or Famine?
Nuclear Weapons
Population Growth
The Energy Crisis

Frontispiece: Preparing the morning meal, Somalia, East Africa.
Cover: Weeding the ground before plowing, the Punjab, India.

First published in the
United States in 1987 by
Rourke Enterprises, Inc.
Vero Beach, FL 32964

Text © 1987 Rourke Enterprises, Inc.

Library of Congress Cataloging-in-Publication Data

Gibb, Christopher.
  Food or famine?

  (World issues)
  Bibliography: p.
  Includes index.
  1. Famines – Africa.   I. Title.   II. Series:
World issues
HC800.Z9F335 1987   363.8′096   87–12741
ISBN 0–86592–279–9

Phototypeset by Kalligraphics Ltd., Redhill, Surrey
Printed in Italy by Sagdos S.p.A., Milan

Contents

1. Myths about hunger   6

2. The African crisis   14

3. Poverty among plenty   24

4. North – South   33

5. A time for change   41

6. What can I do?   45

Glossary   46

Books to read   47

Further information   47

Index   48

1
Myths about hunger

"The world has enough for man's need, but not for man's greed."

Mahatma Gandhi

"I'm starving!" How often do you say that after a long morning at school, or perhaps at the end of a game of tennis or an invigorating walk? You don't mean that you're really starving. It would just be nice to have something to eat. And the answer to your problem, if you are lucky enough to be from the "right" background, and living in the "right" part of the world, need be no farther away than the school cafeteria or the nearest supermarket. Tragically, for 500 million human beings born in the "wrong" part of the world, the answer is not so simple.

This is what happens to you if you are really starving. When food supplies first start to run out, you suffer from severe and racking pangs of hunger. These do not last, however, and in a few days the pains will go. To find the energy to walk about and search or beg for food, you are now reliant on your reserves of body fat. Depending on how fat you were when the food first ran out, these reserves may last a week or two, perhaps three – but in the end they will be exhausted.

The only option left to your body now is to use up the energy reserves contained in your muscles. This process leaves you listless and depressed, too tired to do anything very much. Around you, people, particularly young children, will be starting to die. As your body weight plummets and your limbs become shrunken and emaciated, your personality may start to change. You may fly into impotent and irrational rages. As death approaches, you become apathetic and increasingly indifferent to your fate. This is probably just as well, for starving is a most unpleasant way to die.

Food. Our most basic human need, our most fundamental human right.

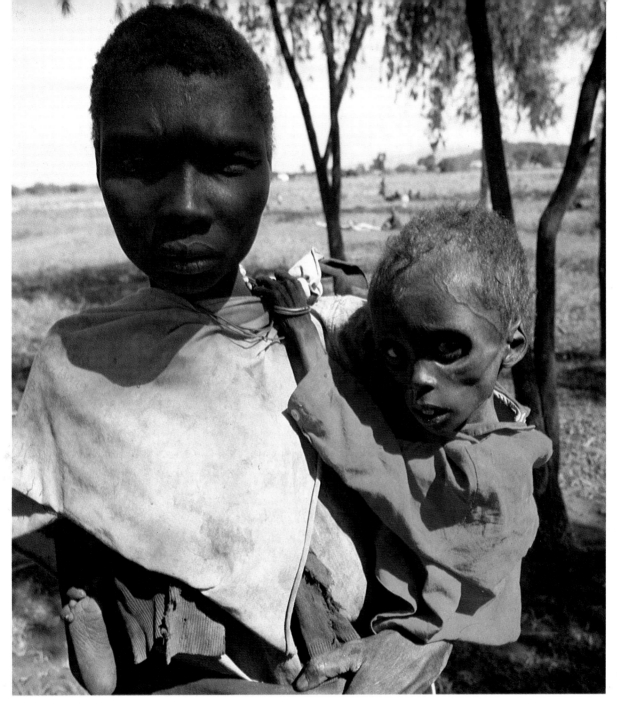

Famine. This is the image most of us have of Africans, but is it true or fair?

That is what happens to you if you are caught in a real famine – when there is no food at all. It is the fate that was suffered by millions of men, women and children in the great famine of sub-Saharan Africa, which is still not completely over. But even when there is no "Great Famine" to dominate our television screens, over 500 million people – that is one-eighth of the world's population – are suffering from chronic, lingering hunger. The number is ever increasing and it has roughly doubled in the last ten years. And, of course, it is the young children who suffer most. Fifteen million of them die from hunger and other related causes each year.

And yet there is no good reason why anyone in the world should be short of food. In 1985, the world produced a quarter *more* grain than it could eat. The problem is that much of this food is in the wrong place, and where it *is* available, the very poor do not have the money to buy it. It is simple justice that is in short supply, not food.

"The Great Starvation"

"From the moment I open my door in the morning until dark, I have a crowd of women and children crying out for something to save themselves from starving. The only reply to my question, 'what do you want?' is 'I want something to eat.' It is so simple, so universal, that it tells its own tale, and neither rags nor sickness, nor worn-out faces nor emaciated limbs, can make their situation more truly pitiable than these few words."

Most people probably believe that hunger and famine happen somewhere else – over there, in the distant and remote two-thirds of the planet we call the "Developing World." All too often, the haunting images of human misery we see on TV or in the newspapers, are explained away as the results of "freaks" of nature – droughts, floods, earthquakes, acts of God. But is this really true?

It is true that famine does not occur today in the richer countries of the world. But it used to. Historians believe that in the Middle Ages, famine swept across Europe as regularly as every ten years. The words quoted at the beginning of this section were not, as might have been supposed, referring to the latest tragedy in Africa. They were written by an

Ireland, 1847: starving families gather outside a workhouse during the potato famine.

observer, George Dawson, of one of the last great European famines, which hit Ireland with catastrophic results between 1845–50. There were many similarities between that disaster and what is happening in some parts of the world today.

As any history book will tell you, the Irish famine was caused by the failure of the potato crop, which was the only source of food available to the country's four million poor people. The potato harvest was devastated by a disease called blight. For three years running – 1845–47 – the staple diet of the Irish rotted in the fields.

A classic "natural disaster"? Well, not exactly. For during the "famine years," Ireland produced food – grains, cattle and dairy produce – in abundance, indeed, enough to feed sixteen million people – twice the population of Ireland. So why need anyone have starved?

Ethiopia, 1985: the people of a famine-stricken village consult with their leader.

The profound comment of our era is that, for the first time, we have the technical capacity to free mankind from the scourge of hunger. Therefore today we must proclaim a bold objective: that within a decade, no child will go to bed hungry, that no family will fear for its next day's bread and that no human being's future and capacity will be stunted by malnutrition.
Dr. Henry Kissinger, World Food Conference, 1974

Over the last decade the number of hungry people has roughly doubled.
United Nations report, 1985

The reason was that this food was transported to the ports, often under armed guard, and exported abroad. For most people did not own the land they plowed and sowed. It belonged to landlords, many of whom did not live in Ireland at all, but in England. In order to pay their rent, the Irish peasants needed to grow crops that they could sell for money – which they then paid to their landlords. Crops grown for export in this way are called cash crops.

Cash crops are cultivated on more than a quarter of the fertile land in the Developing World.

In normal times, the Irish farmers ate the potatoes that they grew for themselves on the remainder of their land, but when the blight came they had nothing. Nor was it possible for them to buy some of the plentiful food around them, for all their money went on paying the rent. If the rent was not paid, they would be turned out of their houses and off their lands. As George Dawson wrote, "There is no want of food in this neighborhood; but it is at such a price as makes it totally impossible for a poor man to support his family."

Unlike other disasters, such as earthquakes, famines do not sweep through whole communities indiscriminately. During the present famine in Africa, it is the very poor who have suffered. Merchants, businessmen and army officers don't starve – however bad the crop failure.

Charity organizations in England did try to do something to help Ireland's miseries. But their aid was often not very effective and sometimes made matters even worse. Irish grain was bought up by relief committees in England and reshipped to Ireland, where it was resold at half its cost. This had the result of reducing the general price of grain, which meant that the Irish peasant had to grow even more to pay his rent. Moreover, by this time, many peasants were completely destitute and had no money to buy grain at even half the price. Consequently, it was bought up by speculators, who reshipped it to England, where the relief

1847: Irish emigrants undergo the arduous journey to the New World.

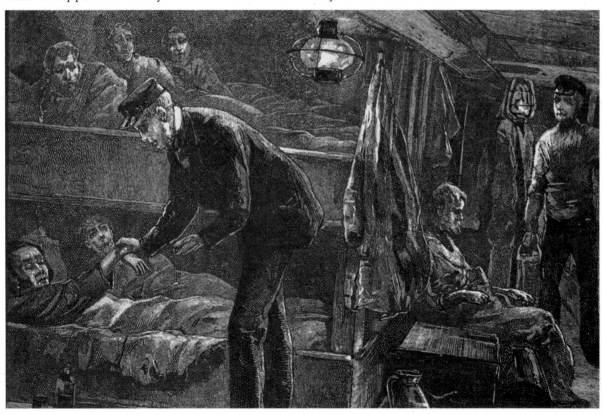

committees bought it for a second time to send it around the circle again and again. Truly, this was a dance of the absurd.

During the famine in Africa, food aid was a lifesaver. But it is not the long-term solution to hunger and, indeed, it can make matters worse by discouraging the local population to grow food for themselves.

Some people maintain that great famines, like the one that attacked Ireland in the nineteenth century, are in the end inevitable because there are too many people. They point to the large size of Irish families and declare that the land was unable to support such numbers. But wait a minute. Remember, during the famine Ireland was producing *twice* the food needed by its population, but most of it was being exported. In addition, very poor people need lots of children to help in the fields and to take care of them in their old age.

Africa has the highest birthrate in the world; yet, according to the Food and Agriculture Organization of the United Nations, the continent's fifty-one countries could feed three times their present population.

1985: Refugees leave their homes in the Tigre Province of Eritrea to seek food and water. Many died on this journey.

When a great famine ends, things do not simply return to normal. The "Great Starvation" was a turning point in Irish history. Death and emigration to the New World reduced the population of the country by a third in ten years. For the destitute of Ireland, leaving their famine-stricken land to sail into the unknown was no safe or easy decision. In 1847, one in six died in the stinking holds of emigrant ships. There is a poignant monument that stands on the shores of Grosse Island, in Canada, which reads as follows:

> "In this secluded spot lie the mortal remains of 5,294 persons who, flying from pestilence and famine in Ireland in the year 1847, found in America but a grave."

The present African crisis has set millions on the move in the search for food and land. Most have nothing, and have left nothing behind them save empty villages and encroaching desert.

What's it got to do with us?

"No man is an Island, entire of itself; every man is a peice of the Continent a part of the main . . . Any man's death diminishes me, because I am involved in Mankind; And therefore never send to know for whom the bell tolls; it tolls for thee."

John Donne – seventeenth-century English poet

It has got a great deal to do with us! Today the world is a shrinking place, and we cannot simply stand by and watch fellow humans be destroyed by avoidable famine. In an age where we can fly around the world in a matter of hours, watch a sports event "live" on TV from the other side of the globe and put a man on the moon, it is a disgrace that we cannot achieve the elementary feat of ensuring that everyone of us receives the one overriding necessity for life – food. Our technology can destroy the world a hundred times over, but

The Developing World has paid a high price to put goods on our supermarket shelves.

we cannot feed ourselves.

It is a lasting truth that we now live in an interdependent world. Go to your local super-maket. There you will find goods from all over the globe – coffee from Kenya and Brazil, tea from Sri Lanka and India, bananas from Central America, peanuts from Mali – and yet, are we sure that these countries are receiving a fair deal for providing us with such luxuries? Over the past twenty years we have, in fact, been paying less for these goods, while charging more and more for our own. Are we also aware of the effect on the environment, and the loss of land, which instead should be used to grow food for their own people, that the Developing World countries undergo to produce these goods? A recent television ad boasted, "Our peanuts are fresh from the jungle." The irony is that peanuts don't come from the jungle. You have to chop the jungle down first to grow the crop, but the land erodes, shorn of its natural forests and their protection. You get your peanuts, but the land turns to desert.

A family collects animal fodder in the rice fields of northern India.

Dealing as it does with famine and hunger, much of this book will be concerned with the starker, more chilling side of life in developing countries. There is a danger here. It is not cor-rect to believe that everything in the Develop-ing World is absolutely desperate – with people everywhere dying of starvation, floods, hurricanes and earthquakes. Such beliefs can lead to a sense of superiority, with "us" raising money to help "them" because "they've" made a mess of things again. The opposite image, of everything "over there" being strange and exotic, of waving palms and glamorous "natives" – as is portrayed in many ads – is equally false.

Ultimately, we are all part of the same human race, and our similarities greatly outweigh our differences. Where differences do exist, they enrich us. It is not a matter of "them" learning from "us" at all. We all need to learn together.

2
The African crisis

"Dawn, and as the sun breaks through the piercing chill of night on the plain outside Korem, it lights up a biblical famine, now, in the twentieth century. This place, say workers here, is the closest thing to hell on earth."

Michael Buerk's haunting words during a BBC broadcast in October 1984, first awakened the world to the tragedy unfolding in Africa. And yet it was no secret. For years, African governments and aid workers had been warning that disaster was just around the corner.

For the average person on the street, the reason for the famine appeared self-evident – drought. But this is only partially true – just as the blight of the Irish potato was not the whole story of the famine in Ireland. Many other countries – the United States and Australia, for exam- ple – also suffer from severe droughts, yet nobody starves. Both India and China were once subjected to terrible famines, yet today they have solved many of their problems. So why are things still so bad in Africa?

The answers are many and complex. Basi- cally, famines occur when people in a country, or area, who can usually feed themselves, sud- denly cannot. The reason they cannot *may* be triggered off by a natural disaster, such as a drought or a flood. But this is not the underlying reason for the subsequent starvation. If crops fail in a rich country, the government will step in to bail out the farmers and buy in food from elsewhere. Even in a poor country like India, harvest failure does not necessarily mean star- vation. Villagers can usually exert enough pres- sure on local government officials to provide adequate relief provisions to see them through until the "natural" disaster has passed. In many parts of Africa, however, the very poor have nobody to turn to in times of disaster. With no additional money to pay for food from other areas of the country – and there always is some food available, however bad the drought or flood – the failure of their crops is a catastrophic event.

Haunted by hunger – refugees at the Korem camp, in Ethiopia.

Above *Africa's dying land, ravaged by drought, overgrazing and deforestation.*

Inset *The growing desert.*

Desert areas

Semi-desert

Life has always been precarious in Africa – particularly in the region directly below the Sahara, which contains twenty-nine of the world's thirty-six poorest countries. However, over the centuries, societies have coped with the difficulties caused by their environments. In some parts of the U.S., for example, people have learned to live with a climate that becomes so cold nothing will grow for several months. They call it winter. In Africa, droughts have always been frequent and the soil poor, yet famine on its present scale has probably never occurred before. Why?

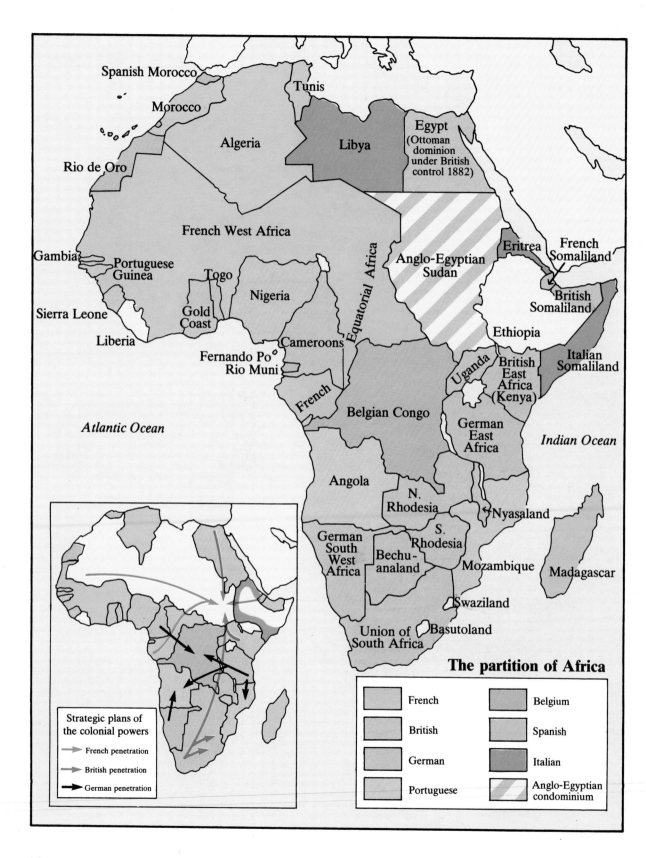

Spanish Morocco

Tunis

Morocco

Algeria

Libya

Egypt
(Ottoman
dominion
under British
control 1882)

Rio de Oro

French West Africa

Eritrea

French
Somaliland

Gambia

Portuguese
Guinea

Anglo-Egyptian
Sudan

Togo

Sierra Leone

Gold
Coast

Nigeria

Equatorial Africa

British
Somaliland

Liberia

Ethiopia

Cameroons

Italian
Somaliland

Fernando Po
Rio Muni

French

Uganda

British
East
Africa
(Kenya)

Atlantic Ocean

Belgian Congo

German
East
Africa

Indian Ocean

Angola

N.
Rhodesia

Nyasaland

German
South
West
Africa

S.
Rhodesia

Bechu-
analand

Mozambique

Madagascar

Swaziland

Union of
South Africa

Basutoland

The partition of Africa

Strategic plans of
the colonial powers

→ French penetration

→ British penetration

→ German penetration

French	Belgium
British	Spanish
German	Italian
Portuguese	Anglo-Egyptian condominium

16

The colonial legacy

"Barely viable colonies make chronically poor states."

Ieuan Griffiths – British geographer

In 1884, statesmen from the most powerful countries in Europe attended a convention in Berlin. Their purpose was to reach a "gentleman's agreement," whereby they parceled out the continent of Africa among themselves. If you look at a map of Africa today, the state boundaries are all made up of straight lines and right angles – none of them possess the usual "squiggles" that represent genuine borders between communities.

Cutting across tribal groups and the smaller, more subtle forms of African community as they did, these crudely drawn boundaries have caused endless conflicts between African states ever since they achieved independence. In 1966, the seeds of disunity sown at Berlin exploded in a murderous civil war between the *Ibo* tribe of Biafra and the rest of Nigeria. Today, there is hardly a country in Africa that does not have some internal conflict or a border dispute with its neighbor. And it is the richer nations, both from the Eastern and Western blocs, that are supplying the weapons that keep such conflicts on the boil. A combat aircraft for thirty million dollars is the sort of toy that no African country can afford.

Opposite *The colonial partition of Africa.*

Below *The Developed World supplies more arms than aid to the developing nations.*

In particular, the conflict in the Horn of Africa has become a hotbed for superpower involvement. Because of its strategic position, astride the shipping lanes close to the Arabian oilfields, both the U.S. and the Soviet Union have vied for influence in Somalia and Ethiopia. An ugly arms race has been fueled in a region that is least able to afford it and at a time when the area has been hit by a famine of devastating proportions. These internal conflicts have obstructed many relief projects and consequently have cost many lives.

The economic legacy of colonialism has also left its mark on Africa. By and large, the colonial powers – Britain, France, Germany, Portugal and Belgium – decided how Africa should fit into the world economy of the time. The most fertile agricultural land was given over to cash crops – crops for export. Kenya would plant coffee, Sudan would grow cotton, while Ghana's climate made it perfect for cocoa. Unfortunately, people can eat none of these things. Meanwhile, Belgium exploited the Congo's (now Zaïre) copper mines for all they were worth. Storage facilities, roads, rail links, administrative centers like Nairobi and Abidjan, were all established, not to bind African society together or to create internal markets, but to facilitate the transfer of her resources abroad. Increasingly, the poorer, subsistence farmers – growing the traditional African food crops of corn, cassava and sorghum – were pushed out into the more infertile, marginal lands. This historical development has been one of the main causes of desertification – the transformation of grazing or arable land into desert – just as much as the population explosion of modern times. As a result, Africa's economy is still today caught in the straitjacket that the continent's previous rulers imposed upon it.

After independence

"Starve the city-dwellers and they riot; starve the peasants and they die. If you were a politician, which would you choose?"
Relief worker in the Sahel

At the time of independence, a general mood of optimism prevailed in Africa. It was rapidly to turn sour. When the European powers left, their place was often taken by rich, black "elites," some of whom became corrupt, many of whom all too frequently continued the policies of their predecessors – though it must be said, many had little choice. In Nigeria, it was widespread corruption that provoked the new-year coup against the regime in 1983. The rot reached the pinnacle of power in Zaïre, whose President Mobutu is reported to have over 250 million dollars stashed away in Europe – this in a country where the average earnings per head of the population is less than 190 dollars per year.

When we arrived, there were about 60,000 starving people in Korem camped in an open field outside the town. There was almost no food, and no real shelter, and the nights up there are cold, with temperatures falling to around zero. The early morning scenes were the worst, by far the worst thing I have ever seen. There was this tremendous mass of people, groaning and weeping, scattered across the ground in the dawn mist. I don't really know how to describe it, but the thing that came to my mind at the time was that it was as if a hundred jumbo jets had crashed and spilled out the bodies of the passengers amongst the wreckage, the dead and the living mixed together so you couldn't tell one from the other.
Mohamed Amin – TV cameraman

However, the problem goes much deeper than the honesty of some African leaders. At independence, most African nations found themselves left with only one or two commodities, usually export crops or minerals, that they could sell on the world market to earn foreign exchange – pounds or dollars. They need this money to buy the goods that they don't produce themselves, such as oil, machinery, fertilizer and motor vehicles, and also to pay off the interest on loans made to them as "aid" by richer countries. To ensure that there are enough cash crops both for export and to keep the people of the main towns happy (for this is where the politicians have their power bases), African governments rely on multi-

A tea plantation in Burundi, Central Africa. Cash crops often use up much-needed fertile land.

national companies that ignore food crops and take over the best land. These companies may stake out large plantations, or they may persuade small farmers to set aside half their land to grow cotton and coffee. Whichever way it is done, it means less land for growing food – just like in colonial times.

This concentration on cash crops and foreign exchange has caused a deep division in African society between city-dwellers and richer farmers, and the 70 percent of Africans who subsist on the land. African governments have ignored their rural poor and have spent their money filling their cities with hotels, factories, cars and universities. And in carrying out these policies they have been advised, financed and assisted by northern governments and aid

19

organizations. The result is a veneer of glitter in the cities – expensive cars full of civil servants, businessmen, soldiers and policemen, a few factories producing goods the majority cannot afford, and a number of plush new hotels full of aid experts – yet, all around, the countryside decays. And as rural society collapses, so increasingly the false glitter of Africa's capitals is surrounded by slums, as the destitute move from the country to the city.

When a drought occurs, it is the neglected, rural poor struggling to survive on the marginal lands who are the first to suffer. Richer farmers, who may have received government money to install irrigation systems and buy fertilizer (so eager are governments to produce the crops that bring in the dollars) are in a much better position to "weather the weather." Indeed, during the drought in Mali between 1967–72, cotton production actually *increased* by 400 percent – some people, at least, had money to buy food.

Overall, the policies of African governments, encouraged by the richer northern nations, have been a disaster. Over the past twenty years, the value of cash crops on the world market has been declining. In 1965, about three tons of West African bananas were needed to buy one tractor. Today, the same tractor would cost nearer twenty tons. At the same time the cost of machinery, fuel, fertilizers, and all the other things African countries need (and which we're so eager to sell them), have in some cases risen by as much as 100 percent. The only answer for the Africans has been to borrow. To pay off their debts, more cash crops are needed – and so the cycle of poverty continues. These problems of trade and debt are common not only in Africa, as we shall see later. Meanwhile, who are Africa's rural poor?

Nairobi, the capital of Kenya. A city of great beauty, but what about the surrounding country?

The African farmer and her husband

"I can see for myself that they are tired, that they work too hard. But tradition stops us from helping them. It is women's duty to work more than men."

Male peasant – Burkino Faso

As your mother has undoubtedly told you, women generally work harder than men. In Africa they work hardest of all.

For in Africa, it is the women who are the farmers. Over 70 percent of all agricultural work is done by them, yet they have been largely ignored by both governments and aid experts. Despite bearing the burden of family survival, most women do not own the land they cultivate, nor do they have the right to apply for credit or other financial services to improve their lot.

In the sub-Saharan country of Burkino Faso, the sheer volume of a woman's workload is staggering. On an average day, she may spend four hours fetching water, two to three hours pounding grain, and an hour gathering firewood – all this *before* any work is done in the fields. And, if this were not enough, she may have up to half-a-dozen children to contend with as well. The men in Burkino Faso do their share of planting and harvesting, but as the above quotation suggests, tradition (primarily Muslim tradition in this part of Africa) prevents them from assisting with domestic chores. "The work never seems to be finished" is the despairing cry of a mother of four.

The story is similar in other parts of the continent. In Senegal, the women grow all the rice; in Zaïre, four-fifths of the food is cultivated by female hands; and in Botswana, men limit themselves to the plowing only.

Part of the reason for this woman's burden is cultural, as in Burkino Faso. But it goes deeper than this. Before the Europeans arrived, many African communities did have traditions of sharing in work, land and marriage. African society, however, was severely disrupted by the economy that the outsiders wished to impose on the continent. Labor was needed to tend the new plantations and to work the mines. Men were enticed away from their villages by promises of wages and the glitter of city life.

The African woman's burden: mother, worker, servant. She has few rights in most African countries.

They were encouraged to turn their backs on the land, with its unending struggle. Today, this trend continues. Men continue to migrate to the cities to escape the poverty and stagnation of the countryside, leaving their families behind them. The lucky ones who find work may send back money. Many find nothing and end up in the burgeoning shanty towns. Meanwhile, in the villages, two out of five women have no man to help them.

Even when the men stay, the womenfolk have little say over the use that the land is put to, for they do not own it. In Kenya, large sugar companies have persuaded many men to give up growing corn and to grow sugar instead. The enticement is the hard cash they will soon have in their pockets. But this doesn't help the women. As one of them complained bitterly,

"When men have money in their pockets, all they want to do is drink beer and go with prostitutes." Nor does it lessen their workload. While the sugar company provides tractors for plowing and harvesting, all the weeding still has to be done by hand and that is "woman's work." Meanwhile, the corn supplies begin to run low and the men have spent all the money.

Before any real change can take place in Africa's food situation, more attention needs to be paid to those who carry the burden of its production. So far, the United Nations has spent a paltry 0.5 percent of its agricultural aid on projects for women. Meanwhile, in the words of the Ugandan poet, Okot p'Bitek:

Woman of Africa
Sweeper
Smearing floors and walls
with cow dung and black soil
Cook, ayah, the baby on your back
Washer of dishes,
Planting, weeding, harvesting
Store-keeper, builder
Runner of errands,
Cart, lorry, donkey . . .
Woman of Africa
What are you not?

As dusk falls there is still work to be done, fetching and carrying water.

Africa uprooted

"What's the point? Even if you feed me today, I shall be dead tomorrow."

Ethiopian famine victim

The colonial past, the burdens of debt and trade, poor planning and the neglect of the countryside have all culminated in producing Africa's present plight. Nature provided the knockout blow. In 1981, the rains first failed in Ethiopia's highlands; in 1983 and 1984, they failed across the great sweep of sub-Saharan Africa. As crops failed, food prices soared; as fodder disappeared, both animals and people began to starve.

With the threat of hunger increasing, families reacted in similar ways. When the crops failed, some men set off for the towns, hoping to find work and send money home. Others sold jewelry, then tools, and lastly their precious animals. Only when all these things were gone and there was no seed left to plant, did people start to abandon their villages.

From 1983, famine began to spread across Africa like ripples on a pond. As hungry refugees arrived in towns, food became even

Food is distributed to refugees at the Korem camp, in Ethiopia. Food aid, however, is not a long-term solution to Africa's famine problems.

scarcer and more people were affected. Thousands died quietly on the parched and cracked hillsides, far from help of any kind. The lucky ones made it to the camps, but there was nothing like enough food or medicine to cope with the floods of people that were now arriving. In 1984, for example, the number of people at the Wad Sherife camp in eastern Sudan grew from 5,000 to 35,000 in a few days.

Only after the horror of the camp at Korem appeared in our living rooms, did a guilty world wake up to the magnitude of the tragedy and start to act. Today, many immediate victims have been saved. But what of tomorrow? Or are the African people to be forever poor, hungry and uprooted – as in the words of a South African song:

Copper sun sinking low
Scatterlings and fugitives
Hooded eyes and weary brows
Seek refuge in the night
They are the scatterlings of Africa.

3 Poverty among plenty

Asia's struggle

Asia possesses two-thirds of the world's population and only one-third of the world's land surface. As a result, hunger and famine have existed among its multitudes for centuries. It is instructive to compare how two vast countries – India and China – have coped with the problem over the last two decades.

India

On paper, India seems to have made great strides since it gained independence in 1947. Commentators sometimes offer the country as a shining example of success when discussing how badly things have gone wrong in Africa. India, they point out, has a population of about 740 million and a land area only one-third larger than the Sudan, with its population of 21 million. India feeds herself. Sudan does not, and has no prospect of doing so in the near future.

It is true that India now grows more food than her people need. The country has also tried to introduce programs and reforms designed to improve its people's health and diet. Consequently, India has not suffered a famine of African dimensions in recent years. And yet, according to a recent United Nations survey, 190 million Indians still live in near-famine conditions. Just as in Ireland, famine and abundance can exist side by side.

They have a saying in India, "Oh God, let me be born in the Punjab next time." For, with mechanized farming methods producing bumper crops of wheat year-in and year-out, this northern province has become the bread-basket of the nation. So great was the harvest in 1985, that the state warehouses could not cope with the surplus. Yet, a mere 180 miles to the south, in the state of Rajasthan, food and water are scarce and underemployment is high. The same is true in the eastern provinces of Bihar and Orissa, where many peasants survive on coarse grains, wild roots and leaves. So why does the excess grain not go to where it is needed?

It must be said that transporting grain around India is not easy, particularly when the Indian government, like all those of the Developing World, is desperately short of cash. However, corruption, inefficiency and the lack of a real political will to solve the problems of hunger, seem to be convincing reasons behind the inequality of food distribution. There has always been hunger in India and the nation's politicians have a tendency to accept this as part of their way of life. Until such attitudes change, India will continue to store her surplus grain while her people starve.

Rich man, poor man. The caste system is often blamed for perpetuating poverty in India.

However, even if this surplus were distributed to the needy, it would still not solve one of the main underlying causes of Indian poverty – the unequal distribution of land. For, in India, the top 22 percent of landowners hold 76 percent of the land – a figure that has not changed for twenty years. It tends to be these landowners who determine agricultural policy and

Small farms need help to solve the present inequalities in Indian food production.

who also cream off any subsidies that the government may be dishing out for land improvements. By mechanizing their farms, they increase their profits and they are able to buy up even more land. Poor farmers and landless peasants are on the increase in India. The goverment has attempted to enact some land reforms, but for the most part they have changed very little. One reason for this is that the majority of rural people cannot read or write. Consequently, they have no way of enforcing their legal rights and often they are unaware that a law even exists.

India, with its colorful history and great culture, has enormous potential. What is needed is the political will to change.

China

No other country in the world has suffered for so long, and from such devastating famines, as China. For 4,000 years, the Chinese farmer has attempted to scratch a living from his tired land. With over 20 percent of the world's population – nearly a billion people – occupying only 8 percent of the world's cultivable land, China today should be a recipe for disaster. In fact, it is quite the reverse. Modern China is an Asian success story.

Real change did not take place in China until after the Communists achieved power in 1949. The revolution that followed was lengthy and often violent, but it did manage to impose real land reform and to abolish the system of debt and rents that had kept so many millions of families in poverty for so long. Today, the vast majority of the population are fed, clothed, housed, educated and medically cared for. This is no mean feat, given the state of China less than forty years ago.

It can be argued that the price the Chinese have paid for improved living conditions has been less personal freedom. But nobody can deny that the people are better off than before the revolution. Chinese cities and markets may not be as colorful or as interesting as those in India, but in China everyone looks well fed and most people can read. With the more relaxed attitude of the present Chinese regime, even China's "drab" image may be changing.

Self-sufficiency in action. A thriving market at Yumran, in China.

Land for the people – Latin American poverty

Beans means exploitation. A family at work on a soya plantation in Brazil.

In an ideal world, Central and South America would be most pleasant places to live in. The land has great promise, both for agriculture and industry, and at present it supports a relatively small population. Indeed in bygone ages, the native Inca and Aztec peoples enjoyed food surpluses.

Today, unhappily, the vast majority of the continent's population are poor and malnourished. As we saw earlier, one of the problems in India is the concentration of most of the country's land in the hands of a few landowners. In Latin America this trend is even more marked. In northeast Brazil, for example, 9 percent of landowners now possess more than 80 percent of the land. A recent survey estimated that up to 70 percent of the population of that

There is no real concern for the poor in India.
Senior government official

The wealthiest 20 percent of the population of Brazil now has an income that is thirty-three times greater than that of the poorest 20 percent – the widest income disparity of any country in the world.
Recent Oxfam report

In the richest country in the world, to be poor is to be a failure – an outcast to be denied decent housing, a good job and a sense of self-respect.
Recent TV news report

same region was underfed. Yet Brazil, like India, is a net exporter of food.

As with Africa, an understanding of the past history of the continent goes a long way toward explaining its present predicament. Following the "discovery" of the New World by Columbus toward the end of the fifteenth century, Portuguese and Spanish adventurers defeated the local people and parceled out the land into large estates. Tenants were often given small plots of land on these estates in return for providing cheap labor for their landlord.

During the present century, some countries have managed to enact land reforms that have helped the poor – in Mexico, Bolivia and Cuba for example. But, for the vast majority, the pattern of large landholdings remains and has, in fact, grown worse. For over the past one hundred years, many landlords, particularly those in Brazil, Colombia and Central America, have evicted their tenants from the land altogether to make way for large, commercial plantations that grow cotton, coffee, bananas, sugar or raise beef cattle – the cash crops of Latin America. These crops are intended for the expanding cities, or are sold abroad to the countries of the Developed World. The result has been a huge increase in landless peasants, either wandering the countryside in search of seasonal work, such as harvesting, or joining the ever-increasing legions of the poor in the cities. Indeed, about half the population of Latin America now live in the towns and cities – the majority of them huddling in flimsy shanty towns beneath the skycrapers.

Cocoa beans in abundance. The workers, however, receive only a poor living in return.

Imagine living in this South American shanty town, without electricity or water supplies. Little is done to help the residents.

Even if a Latin American government does want to bring about change, it is very difficult for it to do so. The landowners have carved out a very powerful position for themselves in their society. Not only do they own the land and its produce, but they also usually control the distributors, local industries and banks as well. They normally have close ties with the army, which often exists to keep them in power. Consequently, peasants standing up for their rights can expect to encounter extreme violence. The bloody eviction of the Amazon Indians to make way for ranches and plantations is one of the most infamous examples.

Latin American governments also have the richer nations to contend with, particularly the United States. The Americans regard South and Central America as very much within their "sphere of influence." All too often they seem prepared to support military dictatorships rather than encourage reforming governments, for fear that they might smack of "Communism" or "Soviet influence." In Chile in 1979, for example, the U.S. secret service helped to topple the freely elected, reforming government of President Allende, and to set up an army dictator, General Pinochet, in his place. Today, the reforming government of Nicaragua, which has been praised by the United Nations for its efforts to feed, educate and provide medical care for its people, is under constant threat from the American-based guerrillas, the contras, who are bent on overthrowing the regime.

For real help to reach the hungry of Latin America, a fundamental change in attitudes is needed both within and outside the continent.

The powerhouse of food production – the United States

Give me your tired, your poor
Your huddled masses yearning to breathe free.
The wretched refuse of your teeming shore.
Send these, the homeless tempest-tost to me.
I lift my lamp beside the golden door . . .
Emma Lazarus: on the Statue of Liberty

In July 1986, New York held a "party" to celebrate the renovation of the Statue of Liberty and to remember the millions who left Europe to seek a new and better life in the United States. From Eastern Europe, Germany, Italy and Ireland they had come, to join the great "melting pot" in the New World. And many did find a new and better life. Today, the U.S. is the richest and most powerful nation in the world. It is also an extremely efficient food-producing machine.

In the U.S., you can buy strawberries in January, and oranges and lettuces all year round. In Kansas, underground heating enables asparagus to be grown in unfrozen soil in December. One combine harvester in California can pick over fifteen tons of tomatoes in an hour, a job that previously needed a hundred men. In "Egg City" near Los Angeles, a factory containing two million egg-laying hens provides the city with its daily breakfast.

Most American farms are highly mechanized and efficient. They are run more like factories than traditional farms. In fact, many traditional, family-owned farms can no long compete with the large farms owned by corporations, and more and more farmers are losing their farms – and homes – ever year.

The great prairies of the Midwest produce far more grain than America needs. Some of this surplus is sold or given to poorer countries as "aid," though not always with the most charitable of motives or results (see page 36). In other parts of the Midwest, beef cattle are fattened for market on grain. They are also fed soybeans and peanuts (two of the most nutritious crops) imported from poor countries. Half the world's fish catch also provides food for animals.

In this land of plenty, most Americans eat

very well – often too well. Overeating is one of the leading causes of death in the Developed World. Yet, not everyone in the U.S. has the

Opposite *The landscape of central U.S., the heart of the country's grain production.*

Below *The renovated Statue of Liberty, July 1986. Still a symbol of hope to the poor and oppressed?*

chance to die in this way. Even here, among the mountains of abundance, hunger stalks.

While most of the American nation was congratulating itself in front of the Statue of Liberty, another group, consisting of blacks, Puerto Ricans, Hispanics and American Indians, were holding their own meeting to protest at the continuing social injustice in the country. For it is these minorities that form the underclass of the nation's cities. As President Reagan's welfare cuts continue to bite, more and more of the very poor have nowhere to turn to but the streets and the soup kitchens. In the richest country in the world, officials estimate that about twenty million people exist on a diet that the United Nations considers insufficient.

The forgotten people of American society. A line forms outside a soup kitchen in Washington, D.C.

4
North-South

"People who respond with a sort of convulsive emotion to dying children have got to realize that their money can be better spent improving the lot of those children *before* they get into such an awful state – before they become terribly malnourished and on the brink of death."

Lloyd Timberlake – Earthscan

In Western Europe, North America, Australia and New Zealand, the response of the public to the first televised pictures of the Africa famine was unprecedented. In Britain alone, both the Save the Children Fund and Oxfam raised over $3 million each within a month. Oxfam America, a Boston-based organization, has raised and spent $4.5 million in Ethiopia since 1985. Nor did things stop there. "Compassion fatigue," a malady well known to charities, did not set in as they expected. As one charity spokesman commented, "Many people who call do not even know where Ethiopia is. They don't even know how to spell it. But they are horrified by the tragedy."

If horror was the first reaction of the public, it was soon succeeded by a feeling of anger, in a way that had never happened with any previous disaster in the Developing World. People began to question the policies of their own governments toward Africa and to demand action from tortoise-like bureaucracies. Such feelings are expressed most outspokenly by Bob Geldof who, through his work with Band Aid, did more than anyone else to raise awareness among the young about the situation in Africa. What really angered people, as the scale of the disaster became apparent, was that 1984 had produced a bumper harvest in the West. The European Economic Community (EEC), it was revealed, had a stockpile of almost 10 million tons of grain. Overnight, food aid had become a political issue.

So great was the strength of public opinion that governments had to act. The United States approved over one-half million tons of food for emergency relief. That food, combined with the transportation costs, non-food relief, and medical supplies, totaled $2.8 million. Britain reversed a decision to cut its aid budget even further and promised £5 million (equal to over $7.5 million), two aircraft, and 6,000 tons of food. Many other countries also sent relief. But people began to question whether food aid alone was enough.

We have failed in Africa, along with everyone else. We have not fully understood the problems. We have not identified the priorities. We have not always designed our projects to fit.

Ernest Stern – World Bank senior Vice-president

Africa's problem – Africa's biggest problem – is too many people going around the continent with solutions to problems they don't understand. Many of these solutions are half-baked. But this is not to put all the blame on the North. Some Africans don't understand African problems.

Djibril Diallo – UN Office for Emergency Operations

Food aid

"In 1985, two out of every five Africans in the sub-Saharan countries were living on foreign food."

United Nations Report

While nobody denies the value of food aid in times of disaster, it can be a two-edged sword. The experience of the past has shown that continual donations of food can lead to a situation where poor countries become dependent on it. Large donations of wheat, for example, may alter the local people's tastes; such handouts

will also discourage farmers from growing food themselves, for who can compete with free food? This danger, that emergency food aid could become habit-forming, is especially great at a time when warehouses in Europe and the United States are bursting with surplus grain. Dumping it on the Developing World provides a respectable cover for keeping prices high in the richer areas of the world, and thereby benefiting Western farmers.

In fact, too much food going into countries,

This FAO self-help project, in Senegal, is designed to produce various vegetables during the dry season.

particularly if they are recovering from famine, will retard development rather than assist it. As an Oxfam report states, "It (food aid) doesn't address the basic problem of why food is not being grown where it is needed, and it stops people even considering the issue by allowing them to think that the problem has been solved."

The aid story

"We have not always designed our projects to fit in with the agriculture and climatic conditions of Africa."

World Bank Vice-president

Aid to the Developing World – whether it be food, machinery, training or cash – basically comes from three main sources; the United Nations and its various agencies like the Food and Agricultural Organization (FAO) and the World Health Organization (WHO); individual governments; and Non-Governmental Organizations (NGOs) such as the Save the Children Fund and Oxfam.

Since its establishment in 1945, the success of the United Nations in promoting projects in the Developing World has been mixed. The FAO and the WHO have done much to pioneer long-term projects in agriculture and health that are aimed at the poorest areas. However, many of their agencies are filled with experts on northern crop production and northern industry, so that all too often the local conditions in developing countries are forgotten. Money has been thrown liberally at large-scale projects that have little to do with the realities of the lives of the people (particularly the poor) they are intended to benefit. Dams that displace thousands of people, roads that cut through forest land, factories producing goods few can afford – projects of this sort have been described by one expert as "cathedrals in the desert."

Relief supplies are unloaded from an FAO plane in Niger, central Africa.

More questionable is the aid given by individual governments. The United States, for example, originally donated food aid for two reasons: to create goodwill toward the U.S. and so help to stop the spread of Communism, and to build up markets abroad for American goods. European aid donors have similar aims. The aid, when given, is often in the form of a loan – with interest payments required. It may also be "tied," which means the donor country expects the money to be spent on goods sold by its own companies. Most of Britain's aid budget is spent in this way.

Expensive projects, such as building dams, do not necessarily tackle the needs of the poor.

Moreover, government aid tends to be given only to countries that are friendly to the donor, or whom the donor country wishes to woo. Ethiopia is a case in point. Because of its Marxist government, it receives less aid per head of population than any other nation in the Developing World. This was the case before the famine and it remains true today.

Aid from both the United Nations and individual governments is regarded as "official" and has to go through the governments of the developing countries concerned. Unfortunately, this means that even when the aid has been specifically ear-marked for those in need, it still may not reach them. Funds allocated by the EEC to the fishermen of Niger, for example, were used to construct a factory to produce smoked salmon for Africa's luxury hotels.

The third group in the aid story is made up of the Non-Governmental Organizations. Despite having far less money at their disposal, these organizations have three distinct advantages over the other two forms of aid. They are free from the political bias of northern govern-

No strings? Food aid from the United States is distributed in Uganda.

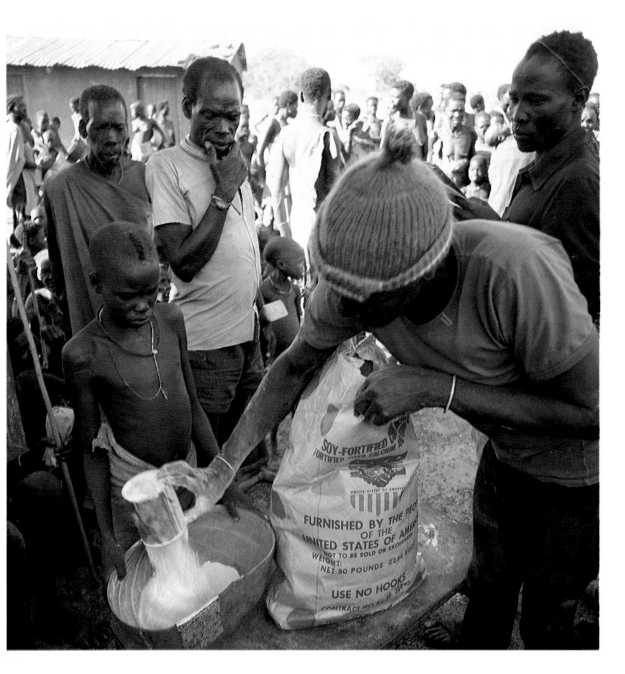

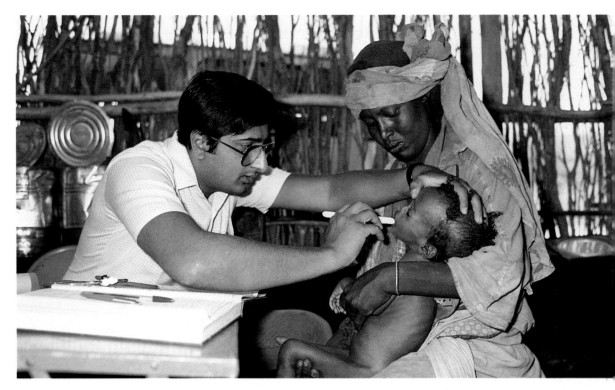

A doctor examines a baby at a Save the Children health-care unit in Ethiopia.

ments; they are more flexible and less bureaucratic than the United Nations; and they are able to spend the money on those in need without it going through the hands of the Developing World governments. While all NGOs are geared to respond immediately to disasters (both Oxfam and Save the Children were in Ethiopia months before the first TV broadcast), their emphasis is on small, long-term development projects aimed at the poorest and the most needy. Save the Children, for example, has been a pioneer in the field of mother and child health-care. By concentrating on introducing basic health facilities at village level, rather than on building prestige hospitals in capital cities, and by always emphasizing self-help among local people rather than imposing solutions from above, they can be sure that their aid is actually working. Oxfam has been even more forthright – championing the cause of the landless and the destitute against greedy landlords, and offering them the chance of a new life by giving them interest-free loans.

Because of their go-it-alone approach and tremendous resourcefulness, NGOs have become extremely successful. Their expertise and grassroots knowledge have made them very influential, and they are regularly asked by their governments to brief them on the local situation in a given area. They also see one of their roles as educating and informing the public of the richer, Developed World about what is really happening in the developing nations and raising awareness for change.

Debt

"Should we really let our people starve so that we can pay our debts?"
Julius Nyerere – President of Tanzania

In October 1973, the price of oil doubled. Two months later, it doubled again. Developing countries, already short of cash because of the falling price of their exports, such as coffee and cotton, were badly hit. Their only solution was to borrow to meet their oil bills.

Meanwhile, the oil-producing countries were making a bundle. They deposited their profits with Western banks, who were naturally eager to lend the money out again as fast as possible. Suddenly, private banks were falling over themselves to lend money to the Developing World. Cash was made available quickly and in large amounts. Because private banks were making these loans, the conditions were strict. Money was usually lent for a shorter period than normal government loans, and the rates of interest were "floating" rather than fixed. This meant that they could go up or down, depending on how the rest of the world's finances were doing. The result was big profits for the banks – but a crisis was approaching.

In the late 1970s, a recession hit the world economy. Demand for goods produced by the Developing World fell even more sharply than before. As a result, developing nations had even less cash. Because of the revolution in Iran, oil prices doubled again in 1979. Meanwhile, high interest rates in the U.S. meant that the interest that the governments of the Developing World were having to pay on their loans went up and up. Many had almost reached the point where they could not pay and it looked as though the entire world financial system was in danger of collapsing.

Prices for commodities such as cotton have fluctuated a great deal in recent years.

Bob Geldof gives a thumbs-up for Sport Aid. He's not so keen on politicians!

Instead of tackling the debt problem themselves, the Western governments decided to let the International Monetary Fund (IMF) deal with it. This body was set up to help with short-term problems in the finances of developed nations. It had almost no experience of dealing with the Developing World. The solution that the IMF imposed was to forbid any further lending to poor countries unless they adopted sweeping "austerity" measures – i.e. "cuts." In countries with no welfare state and with millions of their people already living below the poverty line, the only result of such action is hunger and starvation. Moreover, in order to qualify for loans, the IMF encourages developing nations to increase their exports. This means that today *more* land in the Developing World is being taken over for growing non-food crops than before. As an Oxfam report asked, "Can it be right to make the world's poorest people pay for a crisis that they had no part in creating?"

It is ironic that on the day after millions around the globe had "run the world" for Sport Aid to show that they cared about the future of the Developing World, the UN sat down to discuss the debt problem. Apart from a couple of European countries who offered to waive the equivalent of a few million dollars, absolutely nothing was done to provide positive help. At the time, Bob Geldof expressed his disgust in very forceful language.

5
A time for change

Hunger and famine, and the way the world responds to them, are highly complex issues. There are no simple solutions and, indeed, it is pretending that there are such tailor-made answers that has caused so many problems in the past. In the 1950s and 1960s, for example, Western scientists believed they had cracked the problem of hunger. Agricultural research produced new "wonder seeds" that produced double- and even triple-yields of wheat and rice. These seeds were taken to the Developing World, and millions and millions of acres of land were gleefully given over to the new miracle crop.

But the seeds did not help the poor. For the new plants needed very high levels of fertilizer, pesticide and water if they were to flourish properly. Only the richer farmers could afford these, consequently many poorer ones were unable to compete and went out of business. Richer landowners were able to increase their holding even more, while more families joined the ranks of the rural poor. In India, their produce is sitting in storage silos in the Punjab at this moment. Moreover, it was found that the new seeds had a low resistance to disease. When a blight appeared, it could sweep through an entire crop – as happened to the rice crop in the Philippines in 1971.

The key to solving the world's food problems must be self-help and self-reliance. The poor of Africa, Asia and Latin America could grow the food that they need if we in the richer nations, and the ruling elites of the Developing World, gave them a fair opportunity to do so. Below are suggested some of the paths to self-help development:

Population education, such as the introduction of improved agricultural techniques, is vital if famine is to be eradicated.

Women must be allowed to develop to their full potential in all areas of life.

Above all, communities themselves must be a party to resolving their own problems. Dictated solutions imposed by outside agencies don't work.

2 Literacy campaigns. In India and Latin America, the poor are often exploited and have their land stolen, simply because they do not know what their rights are. When people have access to education they will begin to organize themselves effectively. Slum-dwellers in Peru, for example, have learned how to pool their resources in order to improve their housing, persuading the city authorities to install water and electrical facilities.

3 Credit facilities. Small farmers need to have access to money to improve their land. At present, Oxfam is pioneering many such interest-free loan schemes in India.

4 Women. As we have seen, the half of the population that works the hardest, particularly on the land, has been neglected by Developing World governments and aid experts alike. This needs to be reversed. Where projects have been set up to help women, as in Zimbabwe, the result has been a six-fold increase in food production.

5 Trade. No real progress will be made in the Developing World until the trade problem is tackled fairly by the richer nations. Today the world-trade system has broken down as far as the Developing World is concerned, with its countries receiving less and less for their own produce (which we encourage them to grow), while paying more and more for goods from the Developed World. This trend is often being deliberately encouraged in the West. For years, the EEC has been providing incentives for its farmers to grow sugar beet, which has then been dumped on the world market, thereby drastically cutting the price that the poorer countries can obtain for their own sugar crops. In 1975, the United States bought 100 million dollars' worth of sugar from Brazil; the

1 Small, long-term development projects based on the countryside. As we have seen, it has been neglect of the countryside that has contributed much to the present crisis in Africa. What are needed are projects that are really appropriate to the communities themselves – projects that explain how to make best use of the land to prevent it turning to desert; projects aimed to produce nutritious food crops for local consumption; projects to improve water supplies and irrigation; projects to increase health care, particularly among children.

A doctor from Save the Children at work in Bangladesh, helping to improve health-care facilities.

following year it bought none, but instead tripled its purchases from the Philippines. Such practices keep prices low for American companies, but how can the governments of the Developing World possibly plan their economies? How too can they grow more food crops for their own populations, if they are constantly having to expand their cash crop production to gain foreign exchange? An international agreement that provides fairer, predictable and stable prices for Developing World goods is essential.

6 Debt repayments. At the time of its greatest crisis, billions of dollars are flowing out of Africa each year on its debt repayments. The Developed World *must* work out how interest rates can be reduced for the poorer countries. The United States should take a lead in this, yet so far it has not done so. Indeed, in 1984 the U.S. dramatically reduced its contributions to the International Development Association – the one organization that does supply long-term, low-interest loans to the Developing World.

7 Arms sales. Encouraged by northern countries – particularly the U.S.S.R., the U.S., France, Britain and West Germany – developing nations are spending more and more on weapons of destruction. This is a constant drain on their already scarce resources. Can it be right for us to actively promote the sale of arms to governments that are unable even to feed their own people?

8 Aid. The amount of aid given by rich countries to poorer ones has been falling in real terms over the past few years. For example, Britain's contributions are the lowest for twenty years. More should be given – not to prestigious, grandiose construction schemes for dams and power-stations, but to long-term development programs that really help the poor.

It will not be an easy task to get so much of the world back on the path to prosperity and full stomachs. Both the richer nations and the governments of the developing countries will need the political commitment and courage to face up to change. If we do not wish to live on a planet where one half holds all the resources while the other half starves, this change will have to come soon.

Investing in the future. Education schemes, such as this one in Peru, will give young children the chance to control their lives.

6
What can I do?

"The most lasting way Northern countries can help the Developing World is to change public opinion in their own countries."
Julius Nyerere – President of Tanzania

Perhaps the most important thing any of us can do is to learn – to educate and inform ourselves about the world we live in, and the ties and connections that bind us all together. We also have to accept that development is a complex matter and that nobody has all the answers. One thing is clear, however. Believing that simply digging into our pockets once in a while will solve the problem of hunger is not enough on its own. More fundamental changes, particularly in attitude, are needed.

Each one of us *can* influence these changes. Public opinion, in the West especially, does influence governments and decision-makers. At the back of this book you will find listed a series of books that will tell you more about some of the issues that have been discussed here. There is also a list of organizations to which you can write for more information. Some of these groups run campaigns where you can meet other people to discuss ideas. In this way you can influence more people and spread the message that, in the twentieth century, hunger is unnecessary and that it *can* be eradicated. You can also show a commitment to the world's poor and less-advantaged peoples by helping to raise money for an organization or charity that you know will spend it properly, where it is really needed.

Remember – it is better to light a candle than curse the darkness.

Our greatest enemy is ignorance. By embracing other cultures we enrich our own.

Books to read

Ethiopia by Irene C. Kleeberg (Watts, 1986).

Famine in Africa by Lloyd Timberlake (Franklin Watts, 1986). This author has also written a book on the same subject for adults: Africa in Crisis (New Society Publishers, 1986).

Food for People by Sara Riedman (Harper, 1976).

Hunger by John Scott (Parent's Magazine Press, 1969). Out of print, but still available on many library shelves.

Plants That Changed History by Joan Elmer Rahn (Atheneum, 1982).

Our Hungry Earth by Laurence Pringle (Macmillan, 1976). Out of print, but still available on many library shelves.

Further information

Food for the Hungry
7729 E. Greenway Road
Scottsdale, AZ 85260

Live Aid Foundation
P.O. Box 10923
Marina del Rey, CA 90295

End Hunger Network
125 W. Fourth St., #236
Los Angeles, CA 90013

Oxfam America
115 Broadway
Boston, MA 02116

National Anti-Hunger Coalition
c/o FRAC
1319 "F" St., N.W., #500
Washington, D.C. 20004

Children's Foundation
815 15th St., N.W., #928
Washington, D.C. 20005

World Hunger Education Service
1317 6th St., N.W.
Washington, D.C. 20005

Save the Children Federation
54 Wilton Road
Westport, CT 06880

Picture Acknowledgments

The publisher would like to thank the following for the illustrations used in this book; Aspect Picture Library 6, 7, 14, 22, 23, 26, 30, 37, 38; Camerapress 17, 40; Christopher Gibb 13, 24, 25, 5; Bruce Coleman 20, 36; Mary Evans 8; Food and Agriculture Organization 19, 29, 34, 41; Hutchison Library 35; Oxfam 9, 11, 15, 42; Photri 32; The Mansell Collection 10; The Save the Children Fund 43, 44; Topham 12; ZEFA 2, 21, 27, 28, 31, 39; All artwork is by Malcolm S. Walker.

Index

Africa
  arms supplies 17, 18, 44
  birthrate 11
  cash crops 10, 13, 18, 40, 43
  commodities 18, 20, 38–9, 42
  crop failure 14, 15, 23
  debt 18, 20, 38–9, 42, 44
  desertification 15, 18
  drought 14, 20, 23
  famine 10, 11, 18, 23, 33
  food aid 11, 33, 34
  food production 10, 11, 13, 18
  independence 18
  land ownership 18–20
  literacy 42
  multinationals 18–19
  oppression of women 21–2, 42
  partition 16–18
  population shift 16–18
  refugees 11, 14, 23
  relief 14
  tribal disputes 17
African famine appeal 33
Attitudes to the Developing
  World
  general 7, 13, 36, 38, 41, 44
  superpowers 17, 18, 29, 36, 44
Asia 24
Australia 14, 33

Band Aid 33
Biafran War 17
Botswana 22
Brazil 27–8, 42–3
Britain 33, 36, 44

Cash crops 10, 28, 40
Chile 29
China
  Communist policies 26
  general 15
  land reform 26
  population 26
Colonialism 16–17

Dawson, George 9–10
Debt crisis 38–40
Development projects 35, 37–8,
  42, 44
Drought 14, 15

EEC, the 33, 36

Famine
  causes of 8–10
  general 7, 11, 18, 41
Food Aid 11, 11
Food and Agriculture
  Organization 35
Food production 8, 11

Gandhi, Mahatma 6
Geldof, Bob 33, 40

India
  crop failure 14
  drought 14
  food production 24, 41
  land ownership 25
  literacy 25
  population 24
  poverty 24
International Monetary Fund 40
Ireland
  aid 10, 11
  emigration 11
  famine 9–10, 11, 14
  population 11

Kissinger, Henry 9
Korem Camp, Ethiopia 14, 18, 23

Latin America
  cash crops 28
  colonialism 28, 29
  general 27
  land ownership 28–9
  population shifts 28
  reforms 28–9

Mobutu, President (Zaire) 18

New Zealand 33
Nicaragua 29
Nigeria 18
Non-Governmental
  Organizations 35, 36, 45

Oil crisis 38–9
Oxfam 33, 38, 40

Philippines 41, 43

Senegal 22
Soviet Union 18

Sport Aid 40
Starvation, symptoms of 6
Sudan 24

Technology 12–13
The Save the Children Fund 33
  38

United Nations 22, 35–6, 38, 40
United States
  aid programs 30, 36, 44
  arms supplies 18, 44
  drought 14
  food consumption 30, 32
  food production 30, 31, 34
  immigration 11, 30
  poverty 32

World Health Organization 35

Zaire 18, 22

Glossary

Arms race   The struggle to build up stocks of weapons in order to gain superiority of strength over another country.

Band Aid   A group, made up of leading musicians, that was formed in 1984 by Bob Geldof and Midge Ure, in order to make a charity record in aid of famine victims in Africa. The name was also given to the charity that was formed to collect and distribute the donations.

Blight   A disease that withers and shrivels a plant.

Cash crop   A crop grown for sale rather than to provide food.

Colonialism   The policy and practice of exercising control over another country.

Commodities   Goods or articles that can be bought and sold.

Compassion fatigue   Fading of sympathy and interest due to over-familiarity with a particular issue or problem.

Cultivable   Land capable of being used to grow plants.

Culture   The total of the inherited ideas, beliefs, values and knowledge that are commonly shared by a particular community or people.

Eastern bloc   The group of communist countries of Eastern Europe.

Elite   The most powerful, rich, gifted or educated members of a group or society.

Fodder   Bulk feed for livestock e.g. hay.

Foreign Exchange   The system by which one currency can be changed into that of another country. Some currencies, like those of the larger, developed countries, are more "stable" (i.e. they hold their value over a period of time) than others and are therefore much sought after. The best way for developing nations to gain such currencies is to sell their goods to countries like the U.S. or those of Western Europe.

Guerrillas   Unofficial armed forces, usually with political motives, that oppose a country's regular forces, such as the army or the police.

Hispanic   A person of Spanish descent.

Independence   Freedom for a country from occupation, and economic and political exploitation, by another nation.

Interdependence   Two or more parties (or nations) that depend on each other for their survival.

Irrigation   The supply of water by artificial means (e.g. channels, ditches) to allow the growth of food crops.

Malnourished   Lack of adequate nutrition resulting from insufficient food or a poor diet.

Migrate   To move from one region or country to another.

Multinational   A large company that operates in many different countries.

Non-Governmental Organization   An organization that is involved in an international role, usually on relief or development projects, and is free from government influence in its work.

Poverty line   The point of income below which one cannot adequately feed or clothe oneself.

Recession   A temporary depression in a country's economic activity and production of wealth.

Shanty town   A collection of makeshift homes constructed from scrap material e.g. wooden boards, corrugated iron.

Soup kitchen   A place where food and drink, especially soup, is given to the poor and the homeless.

Sphere of influence   An area of particular strategic or economic importance to a superpower and usually controlled by it.

Sport Aid   A charity run in aid of African famine relief that was held on Sunday, May 25, 1986 in many major cities of the West.

Subsistence farming   A type of farming in which most of the produce is consumed by the farmer and his or her family, leaving little or nothing to be sold at market.

Tacit   Implied or understood without an open statement.

Underclass   A "hidden" class of people whose existence is not officially recognized.

United Nations   An international organization of independent states, formed in 1945 to promote international peace and cooperation.

46